Labrador Retrievers

by Nico Barnes

Visit us at www.abdopublishing.com

Published by Abdo Kids, a division of ABDO, P.O. Box 398166, Minneapolis, Minnesota 55439.

Printed in the United States of America, North Mankato, Minnesota.

032014

092014

 PRINTED ON RECYCLED PAPER

Photo Credits: Shutterstock, Thinkstock

Production Contributors: Teddy Borth, Jennie Forsberg, Grace Hansen

Design Contributors: Dorothy Toth, Renée LaViolette, Laura Rask

Library of Congress Control Number: 2013952556

Cataloging-in-Publication Data

Barnes, Nico.
 Labrador retrievers / Nico Barnes.
   p. cm. -- (Dogs)
ISBN 978-1-62970-033-5 (lib. bdg.)
Includes bibliographical references and index.
1. Labrador retrievers--Juvenile literature.   I. Title.
636.752--dc23
                      2013952556

Table of Contents

Labrador Retrievers

Labrador retrievers are known to be friendly, loyal, and loving.

Labrador retrievers are one of the most **popular breeds**. They make a good addition to any family!

Labrador retrievers come in three colors. They are black, chocolate, and yellow.

Labrador retrievers are large dogs. They can grow to be between 70 and 100 pounds (32 and 45 kg)!

Skilled Dogs

Labrador retrievers are very smart. They can be **trained** to do many jobs.

12

Labrador retrievers make good hunting dogs. Some are **trained** to be guide and **therapy** dogs.

Labrador retrievers have

an amazing sense of smell.

They can help in search

and rescue **missions**.

Exercise

Labrador retrievers are very **active**. They should exercise daily. They like to run and swim.

Labrador Retriever Care

Labrador retrievers' fur sheds a lot! It is important to brush them weekly.

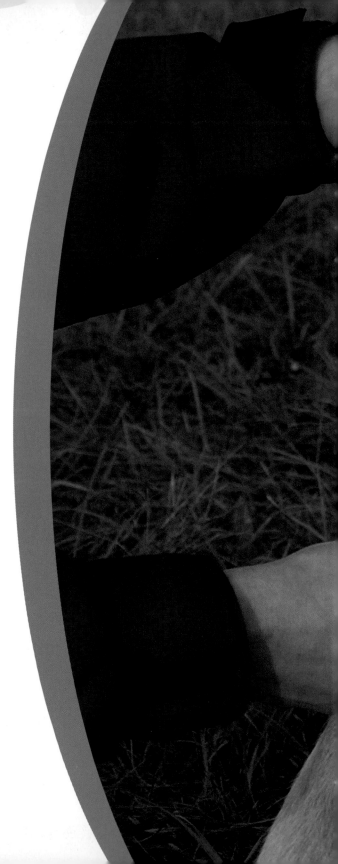

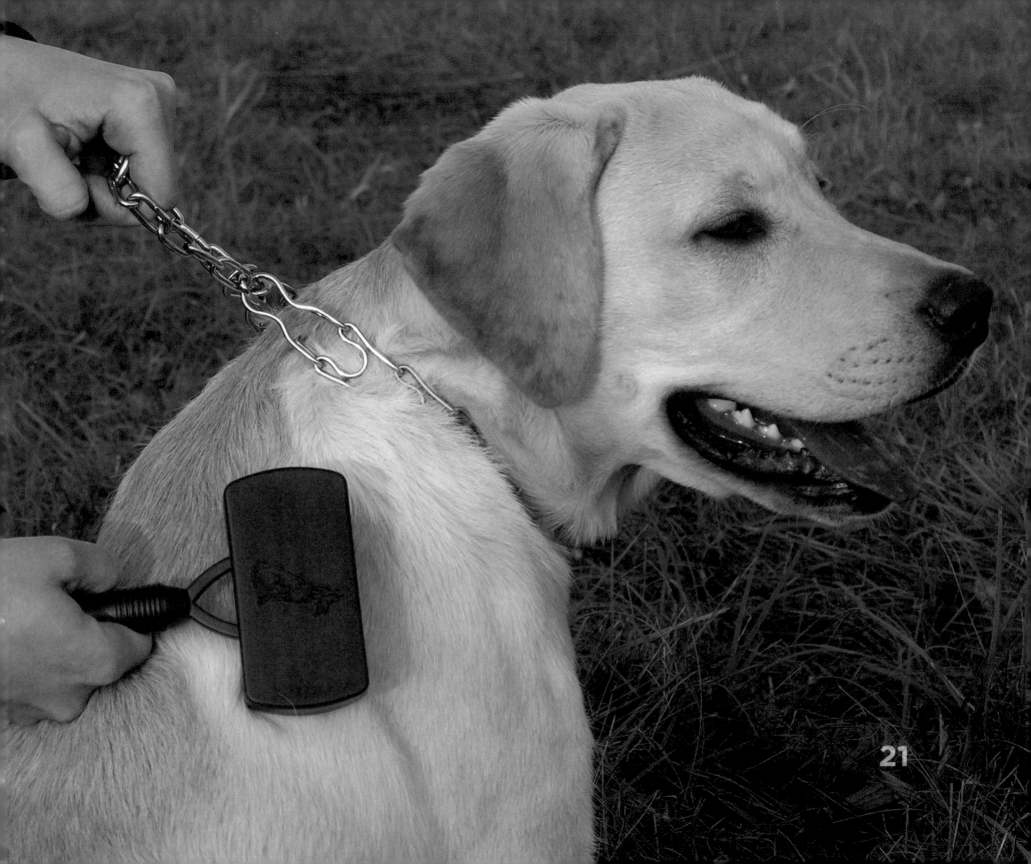

More Facts

- Labrador retrievers instinctively like to hold objects in their mouths. They are very gentle. They can hold an egg in their mouth without breaking it!

- Labrador retrievers have webbed toes. That helps them with swimming and walking on snow.

- Healthy labrador retrievers live about 12 to 14 years.

Glossary

active – busy; energetic.

breed – a group of animals sharing the same looks and features.

loyal – faithful or devoted to someone or something.

mission – special job.

popular – liked or enjoyed by many people.

therapy – a plan for treating problems of the body or mind.

train – to teach to do something.

Index

abdokids.com

Use this code to log on to abdokids.com and access crafts, games, videos and more!

Abdo Kids Code:
DLK0335